Contents

Aaron's Beard	Power	18
Au Clair de la Lune	French Traditional	12
Big Rock Candy Mountain	Traditional	16
Boston Belles	Traditional	28
Can Can	Offenbach	30
Clementine	Traditional	7
Dance Of The Hours	Ponchielli	17
Early One Morning	Traditional	26
Go Down Moses	Spiritual	10
How's Your Father	Power	27
Kum Ba Yah	Traditional	10
Lavender Blue	Traditional	4
Li'l Liza Jane	Traditional	21
Little Brown Jug	Traditional	5
London Bridge Is Falling Down	Traditional	8
Looby Loo	Traditional	11
Mairi's Wedding	Irish Traditional	20
Old MacDonald	Traditional	9
O Susanna	Traditional	25
Quartermaster's Stores	Traditional	22
Skip To My Lou	Traditional	13
Snap	Blackford	29
Sur le Pont d'Avignon	French Traditional	7
The Highland Lassie	Power	32
The Run Around	Power	15
This Old Man	Traditional	14
Twinkle Twinkle Little Star	Traditional	6
When Johnny Comes Marching Home	Traditional	23
Yankee Doodle	Traditional	19
Yellow Bird	Traditional	24

Lavender Blue

Traditional

© Copyright 2002 Chester Music Limited.

Three's A Crowd

Trios that can be performed with any other combination of instruments within Junior Book A.

Clarinet

A mix and match collection of 30 trio arrangements by James Power.

CHESTER MUSIC

Exclusive distributors:
Hal Leonard
7777 West Bluemound Road,
Milwaukee, WI 53213
Email: info@halleonard.com

Hal Leonard Europe Limited
42 Wigmore Street Maryleborne,
London, W1U 2 RY
Email: info@halleonardeurope.com

Hal Leonard Australia Pty. Ltd.
4 Lentara Court Cheltenham,
Victoria, 9132 Australia
Email: info@halleonard.com.au

Order No. PM221462R
ISBN 0-7119-9388-2
This book © Copyright 2002 by Hal Leonard

For all works contained herein:
Unauthorized copying, arranging, adapting,
recording, Internet posting, public performance,
or other distribution of the music in this
publication is an infringement of copyright.
Infringers are liable under the law.

Printed in EU.

www.halleonard.com

Little Brown Jug

Traditional

Con Moto

© Copyright 2002 Chester Music Limited.

Twinkle Twinkle Little Star

Traditional

© Copyright 2002 Chester Music Limited.

Clementine

Traditional

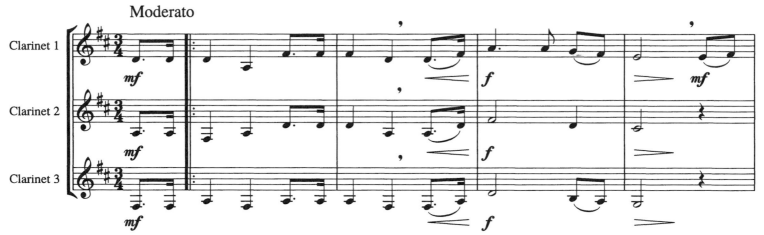

© Copyright 2002 Chester Music Limited.

Sur le Pont d'Avignon

French Traditional

© Copyright 2002 Chester Music Limited.

London Bridge Is Falling Down

Traditional

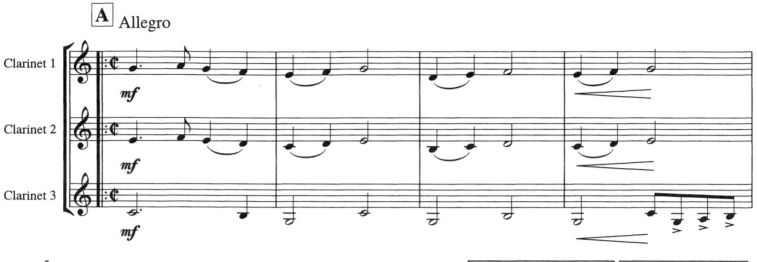

© Copyright 2002 Chester Music Limited.

Old MacDonald

Traditional

© Copyright 2002 Chester Music Limited.

Kum Ba Yah

Traditional

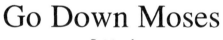

© Copyright 2002 Chester Music Limited.

Go Down Moses

Spiritual

© Copyright 2002 Chester Music Limited.

Looby Loo

Traditional

Rhythmically

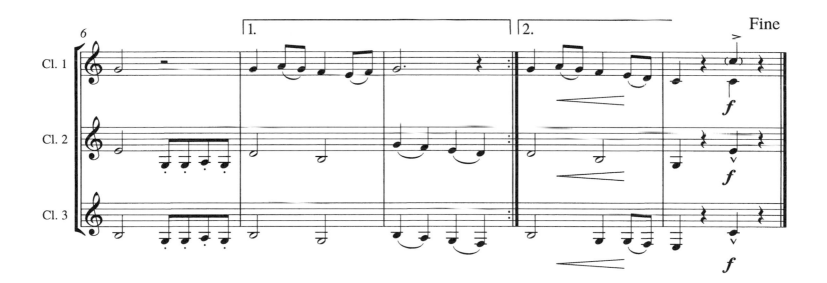

© Copyright 2002 Chester Music Limited.

Au Clair de la Lune

French Traditional

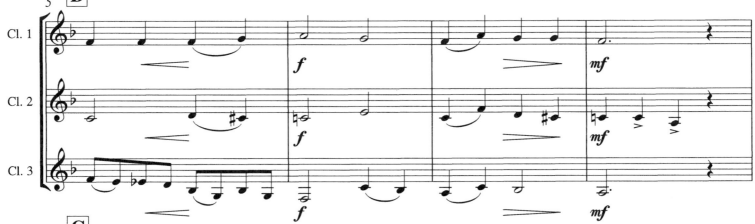

© Copyright 2002 Chester Music Limited.

Skip To My Lou

Traditional

© Copyright 2002 Chester Music Limited.

This Old Man

Traditional

© Copyright 2002 Chester Music Limited.

The Run Around

James Power

© Copyright 2002 Chester Music Limited.

Big Rock Candy Mountain

Traditional

© Copyright 2002 Chester Music Limited.

16

Dance Of The Hours

A.Ponchielli

© Copyright 2002 Chester Music Limited.

17

Aaron's Beard

James Power

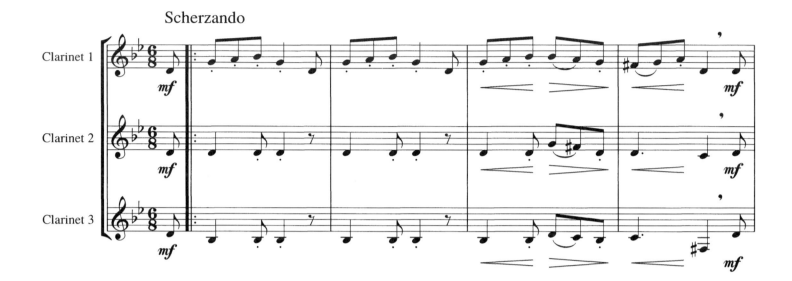

© Copyright 2002 Chester Music Limited.

18

Yankee Doodle

Traditional

© Copyright 2002 Chester Music Limited.

Mairi's Wedding

Irish Traditional

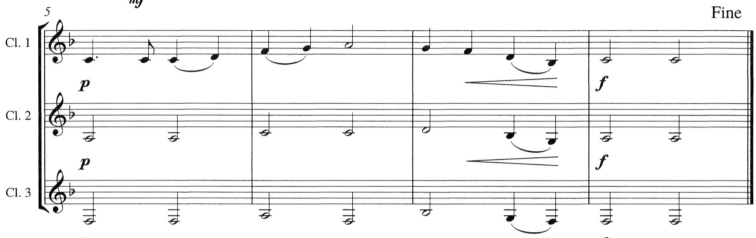

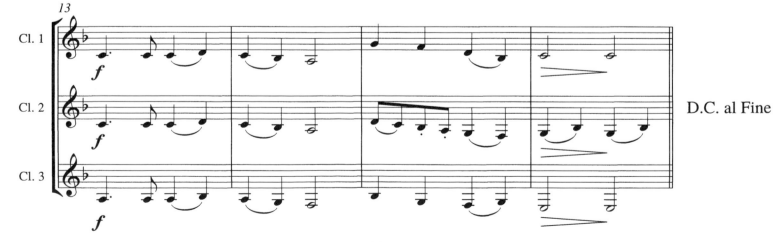

© Copyright 2002 Chester Music Limited.

Li'l Liza Jane

Traditional

© Copyright 2002 Chester Music Limited.

21

Quartermaster's Stores

Traditional

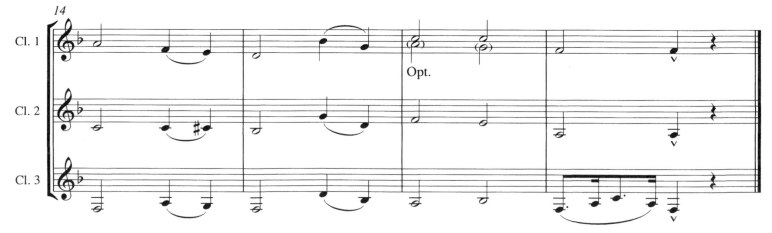

© Copyright 2002 Chester Music Limited.

When Johnny Comes Marching Home

Traditional

© Copyright 2002 Chester Music Limited.

Yellow Bird

Traditional

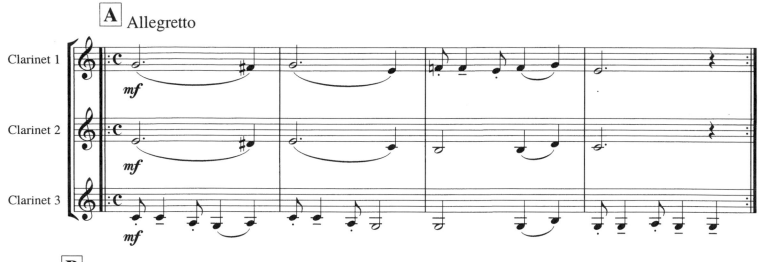

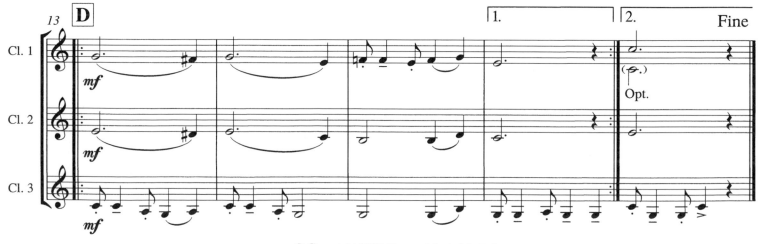

© Copyright 2002 Chester Music Limited.

O Susanna

Traditional

© Copyright 2002 Chester Music Limited.

Early One Morning

Traditional

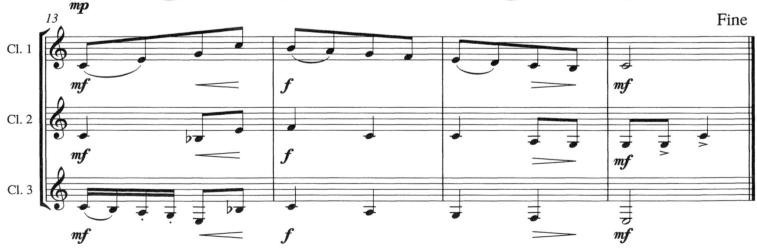

© Copyright 2002 Chester Music Limited.

How's Your Father

James Power

© Copyright 2002 Chester Music Limited.

Boston Belles

Traditional

A

Marcato

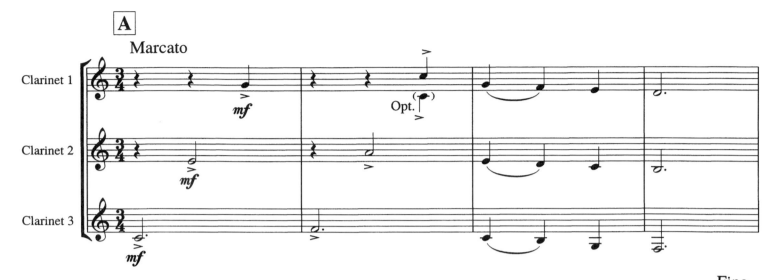

Fine

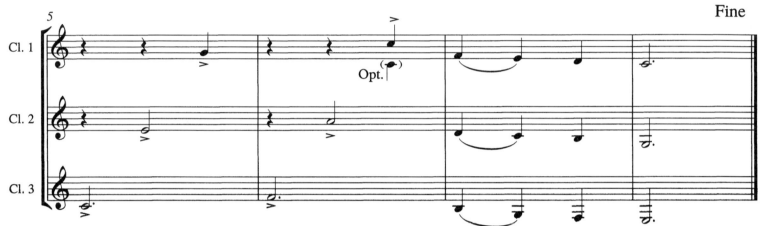

B

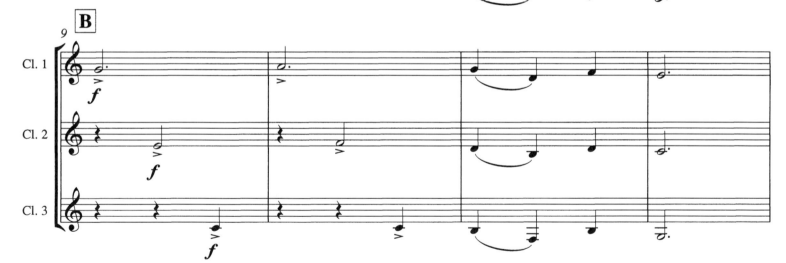

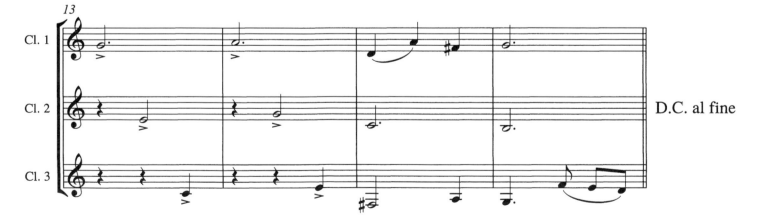

D.C. al fine

© Copyright 2002 Chester Music Limited.

Snap

James Blackford

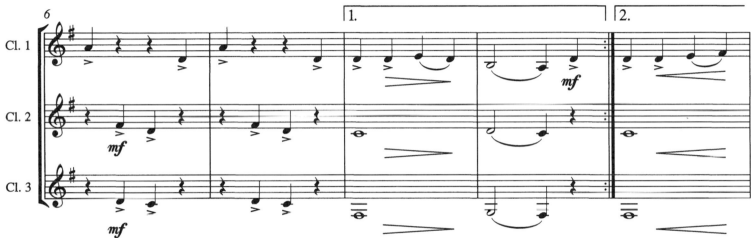

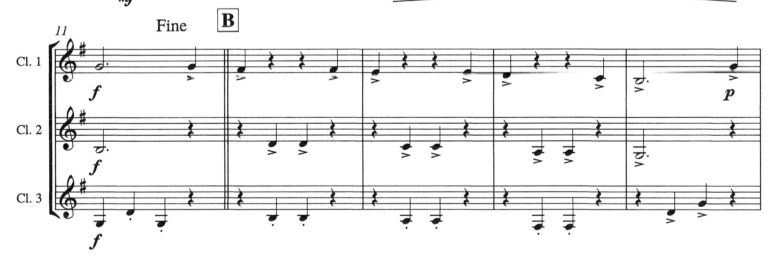

© Copyright 2002 Chester Music Limited.

29

Can Can

J. Offenbach

© Copyright 2002 Chester Music Limited.

© Copyright 2002 Chester Music Limited.

The Highland Lassie

James Power

© Copyright 2002 Chester Music Limited.